Odin's Brew

Óðinsvé at East Coast Thing 2015

Photo by Angela Devin
Óðinn Idol by Josh Rood

Odin's Brew

Voices from the Heathen Northeast

Edited by
Eirik Westcoat & Ned Bates

With contributions by:
Ned Bates
Jill Evans
Stephanie Janicedottir
Laurel Mendes
Ristandi
Mike Smith
Jesseca Trainham
Perris Zoe Weiland
Eirik Westcoat

Skaldic Eagle Press
Long Branch, Pennsylvania
2019

For permissions or other information, please contact the individual contributors or <eirik@theskaldiceagle.com> to get in touch with them.

Front cover photo by Angela Devin
Back cover photo by Michael Morgan
All layout and design by Eirik Westcoat

Collection of August Eve 2019

9 8 7 6 5 4 3 2 1

Trade Paperback ISBN: 978-1-947407-12-1
Kindle Ebook ISBN: 978-1-947407-13-8

Skaldic Eagle Press
Long Branch, Pennsylvania

In Honor of
East Coast Thing

Acknowledgements

The photographers and woodcrafters in the community are also excellent and deserving of renown, and it is an honor to give them some space here in a book devoted to writers and artists. For the front cover photo, thanks go to Angela Devin, but also to Bill Dwinnells, who created the archway in it. In recent years, that archway has been used as the entrance to the Vé-stead at the annual East Coast Thing. For the back cover photo, thanks go to Michael Morgan. He took it at East Coast Thing 2013, when the community was gathered around the fire after the main ritual, and the Gods had given a sign of their approval via the ghostly Thor's Hammer visible in the smoke above. For the frontispiece photo, thanks again go to Angela Devin, and also Josh Rood, maker of the Óðinn idol. The Vé-stead at ECT is a place where people can leave offerings to the gods, and the vés have become quite substantial in quantity and quality in recent years.

Typography Note

The authors use different anglicizations (or lack thereof) for the various names and words from Old Norse and other languages found in the text. No attempt has been made to standardize those spellings across authors.

Table of Contents

Jesseca Trainham

Ned Bates

Jill Evans

Perris Zoe Weiland

Eirik Westcoat

End Matters

Main Editor's Preface

There are many heathen communities (or Asatru communities, if you prefer) of varying sizes and scopes in the United States, and most heathens could probably count themselves as part of more than one such community. With this book, I am focusing on one of the communities that I am a part of, generally referred to as the Northeast Heathen Community. It has organically cohered and grown up around its central annual festival event, East Coast Thing, which celebrated its 20-year anniversary in 2018.

The creativity of this community is one of its best and most vibrant aspects. There are artists, artisans, blacksmiths, brewers, ritualists, poets, writers, composers, singers, musicians, bakers, jewelers, and more. It is fitting that we celebrate and encourage their skills and their creative growth.

I would be delighted to see all of them increasingly honored in the appropriate forums. As leading by example is the only true way to lead, I took it upon myself to contribute to that honor in a way suited to my abilities, and focused on the artists, poets, and creative writers by producing a printed anthology of their works. I have grouped the selections by author to highlight their distinctive voices — each has their own and very different style. The authors, and the pieces by each author, are then ordered in a way that I hope will alternate between smooth flows and striking contrasts. Thus, the individual talents here can be readily seen, even though nearly all of them are published here for the first time. May it not be the last time!

This book is not only a way to honor them, but also the Northeast Heathen Community that we are a part of. It is also a way to give back to the community, first and foremost by the existence of this book, but also monetarily, to a modest degree. Therefore, the publisher proceeds from the first year's sales, minus the costs of publication, will be donated to the East Coast Thing Children's Fund. That fund was started for the purpose of paying for the registration, lodging, and meal costs for all children under 18 who attended the event with their families, and it has grown to support aspects of the programming as well.

Special thanks go to Ned Bates, whose help rose to the level of a strong secondary editor for this anthology. Along with editing and proofreading assistance, he reviewed nearly every aspect of it and gave me numerous helpful suggestions for improving it, some of which I took and some of which I did not. If this volume is less that it could have been, it is probably due to my not taking some of his suggestions.

Finally, my heartiest thanks go to all of the contributors. All of their works appearing herein relate to Heathenry / Asatru in some way. Óðrœrir, the stirrer of inspiration and a gift from Óðinn to Asgard and Midgard, has surely touched the lips of all of them.

Midsummer 2019
Eirik Westcoat

Foreword by Ristandi

As Modern Heathens, we frequently encounter the reality that ours is a tradition of mighty words. Words that build, words that bind, words that we fear can be broken. In our most cherished sacred stories (themselves built word by word), words create and destroy entire worlds. Our spiritual forebears loved riddles, puns, acrostics, naughty jokes, and — of course — poetry. We are the heirs to a legacy that delights in cunning, clever, sweet-sounding, double-(even triple!) meaning words.

Our myths remind us that all poetry is theft — or at least judicious borrowing. Long before T. S. Eliot opined that "immature poets imitate, mature poets steal" (*The Sacred Wood*, 1921), the skalds of antiquity likened the poetic process to a veritable epic of thievery: a yarn of bargaining, trickery, deception, and seduction where — kept word by broken word — the sacred Mead of poetic inspiration comes to dwell once more in the garth of the Gods. But Odin's booty — hard won from Suttung's daughter — is *better* for having been for a while in the worlds of Dwarves and Giants. Kvasir's blood returns to the Gods transformed and rarified — a mightier thing than it was originally. This is part of the mystery Eliot would later confront when he wrote: "The good poet welds his theft into a whole of feeling which is unique, utterly different than that from which it is torn" (1921). And what better way to think about the craft of poetry — or its ultimate goals? We humans, wallowing in mud like Ned Bates' poor little Yipyap, occasionally borrow or steal a little bit of godly glory, the magic that turns the mud to gold, and lets us imagine worlds better, more perfect, more noble than our own.

I've had the honor and the pleasure over the last several years to help organize the Skaldic Competition at East Coast Thing — the American Northeast's longstanding and legendary Heathen gathering. In that capacity, by firelight, with the taste of Odin's mead on my tongue, I've listened raptly to poems, songs, and stories crafted by a whole new generation of "mead-thieves" — those who plunder the word-hoards of the past and brew a new and intoxicating beverage from old sweetness. This — gentle reader — is what you hold in your hands: a unique decoction inspired by ancient worlds but speaking directly to this one, now. Herein are hymns, incantations, spells, stories, cunningly wrought poems in ancient meters, songs to be sung at our holiest of yearly feasts. Herein are words raised like runestones to the memories of the poets of yore — but raised as well to the honor of a new, living, and thriving community of modern Heathens.

I like to imagine Arnhöfði, the Eagle-Headed, the Original Mead-Thief, looking down upon these shining drops, these stolen sips from his full horn that have been distilled anew.

I think he smiles.

Midsummer 2019
Ristandi

Odin's Brew

Ristandi

John Greycap

Author's note: *The following song was written in partial fulfillment of an oath taken at the first International Rune-Gild Moot I attended in Columbus, Ohio. Inspired by several of my Gild-Sibs who were also musicians, I swore to craft four songs in the months following the moot. Most of them were awful. This one — I like to think — isn't. It was an attempt to "reverse" the process explored by R. J. Stewart whereby Pagan lore and practice was preserved in British Folk Song. I wanted to see if I could "encode" Heathen myth/lore in a form that would appear like a traditional folk ballad. I've sung this at a number of festivals around the world and introduced it as the most primal Traveling Salesman joke in the history of the world. Any resemblance to one of Óðinn's greatest exploits is entirely coincidental! This is properly sung to the tune of "King Henry" (Child 32) as recorded by Steeleye Span, but I suspect a number of other traditional airs could suffice…*

I am a rambling cobbler; John Greycap is my name.
I was roving in the North Country and to a farmhouse came.
The farmer was a wealthy man of great and good renown.
It's said he brewed the finest beer in all the county round.

I knocked and knocked on the farmhouse door, and loudly did I cry,
"Will you give some drink to a traveling man; my throat is parched and dry?"
Say's he, "You'll get no ale from me, you'll get no meat nor bread,
You'll work this day in my threshing-house; it's there you'll make your bed."

Now the Farmer had a daughter fine, a buxom lass and fair,
With rosy cheeks and twinkling eyes, and long and flowing hair.
He locked her up in his cellar dark 'til she grew wan and pale.
He made her watch by night and day to guard his casks of ale.

When the sun had set and the owl called and the house was all asleep,
Then I in the cloak of the cold black night to the cellar wall did creep.
The stars were high in the moonless sky, the wind would chill the bone,
And I with the point of my cobbler's awl I dug through earth and stone.

I whispered low to the maiden fair sweet words to calm her fear,
"It's kisses three I'll give to thee for just three sips of beer."
Then three long nights I stayed with her when all above was still,
And many a kiss she got from me before she had her fill.

Then up I rose and donned my clothes and bade the lass goodbye.
I took three hearty sips of ale — drained three full barrels dry!
The Farmer woke in roaring rage and swore he'd have my head,
But the Eagle's wings were at my back and fast away I fled.

Now through the world so wide I make my way; along
the roads I roam
From cavern deep to tavern seat, salt water, and sea
foam.
Lock up your daughters and your ale; I'll have them
both the same.
Let no man quail to tell my tale; John Greycap is my
name!

A Song to Óðinn

Author's note: *This piece was inspired by Rudyard Kipling's "Song to Mithras" (1906), which was also adapted in excellent musical form as "Lord of Ages" by neo-folk band Blood Axis (1998). I've always loved and been inspired by Kipling's incantatory verse, and shamelessly stole the meter and style of the original for what I hope is a comparably inspiring prayer to "Old Stretch" — the Many-Named, the One-Eyed, the Howling God. Rúnar munt þú finna!*

Þundr we call you — the Stretched One! Strung on the storm-tossed Tree!
Bound between baleful Branches and Roots that no eye can see!
Now in the season of shadow, now as the night draws near,
Óðinn — God of the Gallows,
Teach us to tread without fear!

Bileygr, the One-Eyed, we hail you! You who see farther than all!
Eagle-Winged thief of Óðrœrir! Hear us, Arnhöfði, we call!
Now on the edge of the High-Shelf, now where you speak with the wind,
Óðinn — God of the Gallows,
Whisper the Runes to your Kin!

Bölverkr — wicked deceiver! You who turns woe into weal!
Gangleri — wandering wise-one! Grímnir, forever concealed!
Now when the fire is kindled, now when we heave the horns high!

Óðinn — God of the Gallows,
Watch us with unsleeping eye!

Valföðr — Lord of the Barrow! Waker of Draugr and Ghost!
Oskorei, riding the storm cloud, head of the Hell-Hunters' Host!
Now as we come to your Harrow, now as we stand in your sight,
Óðinn — God of the Gallows,
Walk with us here this night!

Birch Galdr

Author's note: *This incantation was written for a private ritual conducted in the early '90s. It was spoken aloud in a Birch grove in Western New York on a hazy summer night when a sickle moon hung in the sky. I was relatively new to serious Runic studies at the time, but the mysteries of Berkano/Bjarkan resonated with my childhood fascination with tree-lore culled from explorations of Faerie traditions from the British Isles, Germany, and Scandinavia (for these I have Nancy Arrowsmith and Katharine M. Briggs to thank!). In the late '80s, I'd already begun to explore the poetics of charm and chant poetry, and this was one of my earliest efforts to employ those techniques creatively. I recommend speaking the prelude, then reciting the poem 3x3 times, at midnight, alone, in a Birch grove, after pouring a libation of strong drink. Leave immediately afterwards. Don't look back…*

Prelude:
Mighty Birch Goddesses! You are the keepers of the wisdom below! Yours are the hands that hold the power of madness and inspiration. Yours is the touch that makes Man into God! Yours the grasp that steals life, and yours the womb that bears it forth roaring and bloody into the world! Long have I ignored you. Long have your runes lain buried within me. I come to you to pay a forgotten debt, to honor you, long left to wait. My power waits beneath like a seed. Oh mighty ones! I come to you seeking rebirth, seeking release, seeking the power of the Birch!

Incantation:

Queens of night,
Ladies white,
Slender ancient powers of Wood,
Waning moon's
Deepest runes,
Yours are secrets borne in blood.

Grasping hand,
God un-Manned
Blessing pours on hungry earth.
Spirits sleep
Drinking deep
Aching for the time of birth.

Rustling leaves,
Silken sleeves,
Fingers touch and madness burns.
Sundered seed,
Burst in need,
From below the might returns.

Queens of night,
Ladies white,
Slender ancient powers of Wood,
Waning moon's
Deepest runes,
Yours are secrets borne in blood.

Laurel Mendes

Invocation to Freyja

Freya,
You are the core of fire at the center of all being.
You are the storm that washes over us in sleep.
You are the heart of our dreams.
You are the lover of our souls.
You are darkness unspeakable and light beyond bearing.
You bring an unfathomable beauty to our days.
You pour out joy like mead.
We would never willingly be parted from you.
Be with us tonight as we praise you, as we feast you.
Hail Freya.

Freyja

As Kvasir's blood once poured forth fully,
We pour forth words of prayer and praising,
From the mighty to the mightiest.
Hostage to her own beauty held fast,
Before ever the Aesir housed her,
Raising her high amidst their own folk.
Revered Dis of the Vanir kin,
Shining brightly, shimmering darkly.

Gullveig's gashes and searings sensing,
Knowing these as her own suffering,
Summoning her strong magics swiftly,
Her weal made war on fire and sword's woe.
Winning her right to choose her own slain.
Gifting peace, well loved by her brother.
Frothi the Frith-God, Lord of Goodwill,
Gains joy from his warrior sister.

Ice and fire fuse fast in her dreaming,
In spells' brewing and seer's seething.
Auguries to the god-mouth she gave;
Odhin's gifts by her hexes heightened.
Old arts flowed from her hands to his;
Ancient wisdoms found his apt hearing.
From thence to the folk they wandered far,
Incantations of elder vision.

The necklace of the Brisings bearing
On her breast, where once four soul-weary
Dwarves dreamed happily, safe, and solaced,
Gifted one night of her thigh's friendship.

Laufey's son tried to steal the secrets
Sealed fast in gold and gleaming gem stones.
Heimdallr foiled the unwise ambition
Of the misguided lust of Loki.

Extol the Seidhjallr's holy queen,
Lauded by Gods, Elves, and Dwarves alike.
High praise to the Vanadis let flow,
From your hands, your hearts, and your mead-horns.
Lady, accept the graces we give.
Let our devotion find you well pleased.
In return, we pray, inspire us,
With the wit to know, to do, to dare.

Feasting at Twelfth Night

I fear I am held captive by an earlier time.

Dreams of ancient festive occasion hold me in sway — feasting on the fine and rare, with wine, wits, and words to meet and exceed the table's offerings — how they call to me.

They inspire me to make that world anew in some small measure, in seasons where merriment was allowed to high and low alike and enforced by higher law.

Somewhere...

...Some-when.

That some-when, somewhere beckons me.

It speaks to me in the night, crying:

"The revel is holy. The celebration marks the passage of days and lends meaning to a mortality of which the Gods can only dream. It is a sign-post in Their immeasurable journey and Their gateway to one moment's passing outside of Their infinity. Their moment to draw one mortal breath.

"And ours to hold Their exhalation in our lungs, that it may fire mind, heart, and spirit and sustain us for another brief span of seasons."

In the silent dark after, the words still sound.

A fault of inattention lets slip the lead by which I hold such things.

Thought runs wild for a stream of seconds, hours, or even days, until I hold fast the traces once more, thus reining in generous, sacred impulse until such time as it escapes me again.

As for me, I do not escape.

I am held captive by an earlier time.

Dreams of ancient festive occasion hold me in sway.

Winter

Dark thoughts, dark words walk the world between
suns.
Time tarries tethered in nascent night's chains.
Sun passes swiftly, pale light leaps lightly
From hillside to heath then hastens away.
Cold walks within doors as much as without.
Fire's faint heat fares not far from the hearthstone.
Still, kind companions soften sad days
And shine some small sunlight into the dark.

Thunder Snow

Mother Hulda will shake her quilt tonight and beat it until the feathers fly. Frost Giants will interfere, troubling the feathers' fall. Thor will thunder them back into better manners. The ferocity of the fray will frighten many, foment fury. Furious action will abound. Thor throughout all will guard the folk. All will end well, the world balanced again.

Seeds

Odhin sets himself the task to ascend
The world tree which will be his spirit steed,
Binding himself to the dark journey's beast.
Pierced is he too, pinned to his promise,
Riding the red blood road, reaching hands out.
Thirsting for air much more than sweet mead.
Hungry for soft stir of sky's sacred breath,
Hands still extended grasping for something.
His heart holding hope, as hands fail to hold.
Elusive, fleeting, life is becoming.
His dream slowly fades,
Life nears to ending,
Nothing calls out to
Nothing remaining.
Nothing to nothing calling forever through time
And through space to time before time.
Hands ever reaching find touch to their joy.
One, then another, falls into his grasp.
Life fades, death falls, all meaning melts away.
Odhin changes Odhin.
Better to grasp.
Runes of great power rest in his keeping.
Screaming he scatters them into the world.

Tyr

Breaking open the world to save it,
The hand of justice strikes his gavel,
Passing sentence from the belly of the offender.
Dissolving into the morass of greed and evil,
The monster's last meal becomes hope made manifest
for all living.
The single-handed feat of the one righteous saves us all.
While the other gods laugh,
The monster's last meal hands the future
Into our keeping.

Hope

Thorgeir, Lawspeaker, a thousand years ago,
Faced his folk, divided by faith, old and new.
Half clung to Christ, the new face of holiness.
Half held to old ways, tried and true over time.
Oaths could not be offered one to the other,
The sworn word sustaining the law of old Iceland.
Thorgeir sought visions, hid under his wolf cloak,
Drew forth the great compromise from his dreaming.
Iceland would now be both Christian and Asatru —
Christian in public and all else in private.
Oaths could be sworn and held by the same God name.
And folk who served old Gods were preserved in peace.

Stephanie Janicedottir

Triple Triangle

Equilateral triangles are not peaceful.
Take the valknot for instance,
Three triangles intertwined as one.
You would think that they are at peace.
A believer of the Trinity would say so.
Those who know Odinn know better.
Valknots demand sacrifice.
Sacrifice of life, sacrifice of stasis,
Sacrifice of self.
Equilateral triangles are not peaceful.

Alas

You awaken before Mani slips into slumber.
Sleepy kiss warm against my cheek. Pillow growing
cold.
A thump thump thumping sound waiting at the door.

A woof and whimper greets you outside.
As you close the door the wind whispers in. Telling of
night.
In the predawn chill, sleep finds my eyes again.

The morning is quiet without you.
The chop chop chopping of firewood absent. Only
chicken clucks.
Your chores were done last night in anticipation of
today.

In quiet contemplation I sit at my loom.
The shuttle weaving over and under, over and under.
The weft hanging down, like the roots of the tree.

Smoke curls up from the fire and drifts in wisps.
A mouse scurries in the corner. The trees shift and
groan.
The fibers of my work rasping as they yield to my
touch.

The wind shifts, and through the window I smell you
before I hear you.
Sweat, blood, and mud come to me on the breeze.
The swish of leaves in the path announces your
footsteps.

A deer dressed with antlers swinging.
A king's mantle over your shoulder. A feast to share.
Our barking hound — the fool heralding your
 triumph.

The animal strung up and forgotten.
You embrace me. Salty lips warm against mine.
Long black locks entangled around fingers.

The musky tang of the earth mixed with your sweat.
I bury my head in your chest. You intoxicate me.
I melt in your arms and the world slips away.

Alas, forest lover, hunter, you are an image not yet
 grasped.
A wish, a hope, a dream.

Spring Irises

You awaken from slumber and open up your arms in
the warm rays of Sunna.
Your perfume is intoxicating.
It floats on the breeze, calling many to your embrace.
Your dress a tease of color dancing in the breeze.
Nectar sweet drips like dew from your petals.
Lips curled back soft, inviting.
The buzz of bees comes with passionate urgency.
Mouths hungry to drink from your horn of plenty.
Proboscis probing into the sweetness of your soul.
Gentle caresses bring seed to fill your belly from absent
lovers.

Soft purple Goddess, let me be your honey lover.

The Dance

Why do we do this dance? I am the shore whose sands shift and change often, but whose place is constant and immobile. You are the sea. Ever shifting and moving. Sometimes calm, sometimes volatile. You come close within reach to embrace me. Then you retreat when the passion and heat of the Sun's rays fade and the Moon pulls you. I wait in anticipation and dread knowing that you will return, but never knowing when.

Why can we not find that place in the woods where lakes hide? To be constantly in flux, but only with fractions of movement. To be encircled by the flora and fauna of the forest, rather than endure the unbridled tidal events of tsunamic proportions that seem to empassion and destroy us.

Why?

Tit for Tat (or The Attic of My Memory Palace)

When you broke my heart, like she broke yours, I may not have acted like you did. I did not confront you in public or display near violent explosions of anger privately in front of my friends, and I certainly didn't let the FB Universe know of my pain. I did not hound you with emails and phone calls long after the deed was done. Instead, I picked up a sledgehammer and walked into the room you occupy in my Memory Palace and began to smash the furniture and tear down the walls until dust caked my hair, blisters formed on my palms, and my fingers bled from scratches.

For days and weeks and months, I've done this to try and scrub the smell and look and feel of you from my mind. Every morning I pick up that sledgehammer and by afternoon the demolition is done. The room is left in piles of rubble and debris waiting to be collected into a dumpster and hauled away. And by sunset, like the Einherjar, every sliver of wood, every shred of fabric, every chunk of drywall makes itself whole again, and day after day, week after week, month after month, the room and its contents remains. And as time goes by I find you have left new objects to occupy and fill your room. More reminders of how I am a stupid, naive, and sometimes juvenile woman to think that there is more to you and me than this hollow room. The room with its treasures that will not and cannot go away. Instead, I try to empty the room of everything so I can start with a fresh coat of paint for someone new. But those objects cannot be thrown away like trash, burned like offerings to the Gods, or donated to those less fortunate.

No, they must be boxed up — my memories and feelings of you. Boxed up and taken upstairs into the attic of my Memory Palace. Boxed up and left to rot, mildew, and collect dust in the dark corners like the other hurtful feelings and unpleasant memories of my life. So when you tell me that my pain has no comparison to yours, you can go fuck yourself and get lost in the attic of my Memory Palace.

Mike Smith

Óðinn

Great god — whirling inspirational fury.
Woð in the forefront of all.
Into Mímir's Well, one-eyed, he sees,
Taking the slain into his great hall.

Wondrous, dark mead — drunk to his fill.
Runic wisdom of the Tree,
Risting forth what is his Will.
The Wild Huntsman, he rides the winds.

Shamanic Óðinn journeys the worlds.
Battles Fenrir for our worlds.
Oversees the slain to prepare them
For the frightening, wonderful…
Rune-Truth.

Runic Rowner

Valknot opens the Knowing
A knife rists forth the Runes
Winds render the Whisperer
Wild comes forth Önd

Óð whispers Óðinn
Overhead the stars Watch
The Rister carves the Roar
Righteously the cosmos Unfolds

Searching for the Found

I'm a tattooed shaman
Left to stone the crow.
I finally found my high-way home
Out by the blood trail, left in the snow.

Listenin' to bird speech,
And chasing dreams,
I finally found my shattered soul
Out by the blood stains, amongst the trees.

Searchin' the stars,
And chanting the runes,
I finally found my lost life and luck
Out by the blood pools, left in the dunes.

The Wilds (A Haiku)

The forest whispers.
Landvættir beckon, "Come."
Never truly lost.

Autumn Rain (A Haiku)

Rain drizzles today —
It's just like Icelandic Úr.
It makes me sleepy.

The Heathen Host

That raucous race,
the Wild Hunt rides!
My quickening heart's pace
and nowhere to hide.

Hounds a' howling,
those fiends fly fanatic;
winds a' whipping,
I pray and panic!

Er' comes that heathen host
as Óðinn's eye shines bright!
So full of ghastly ghosts
riding through never-ending night.

My horse's haste!
Oh, that dire dread!
No time to waste!
Come, O Carnival of Dead!

Jesseca Trainham

Warrior and Serpent

Hail Volund

By hammer and tongs, by forge-fire bright,
By bellows' breath and by anvil's might:
Volund we hail thee!

By shining rings, by keenest blade,
By enemies' bones in the mud now laid:
Volund we hail thee!

On swan-white wings climb the starry way;
Though lamed and captive, yet won the day:
Volund we hail thee!

Volund Takes Flight

Mother Night

O, holy Ladies,
O, ancient Mothers,
Still is the night and the spindle's at rest.
Givers of luck and
Bringers of plenty,
Needful your blessing amid winter's tempest.

O, holy Disir,
Needful your wisdom.
Children go hungry while princes make war!
This Mother Night,
O, ye women of old,
Gather around us that we may know more.

Hands of the Weavers,
the skill of the Spinners,
O, cunning the Healers, the mothers and wives!
The hall is swept clean and
with offerings we call you:
Come to the altar and gladden our lives!

Wide is the Web and
subtle the strands, but
Stronger than steel, binding future and past.
O, holy Ladies,
spin us good counsel;
Weave us together that Erda may last.

The layers of Orlog
Men hardly fathom —
Three are the Ladies attending the Well.
Hearken, good people,
unto the Nornir:
Every unfolding is theirs to foretell.

Live in our hearts and
give birth to the mystery.
Each Night is a Mother, most worthy of praise.
O, holy Ladies,
watch us and ward us,
Lend us your wisdom for all of our days —

Guard us and guide us in all of our ways.

The Holy Mothers

The Yoole-Buck We Welcome

The holly and the ivy bedeck the merry hall
As Tanngrisnir and Tanngniost are the hardiest of all.

The Yoole-buck we welcome, how cunningly he's
wrought!
From hoof to horn of golden straw so that we shall
want for naught.

With ribbons red the Yoole-buck so skillfully is bound,
And red the beard of mighty Thor, whose praises here
resound.

When winter cold oppresseth and hunger sore keen
grows,
Hlorridi takes his beloved goats; for the feast he lays
them low.

And when the feast is ended, he gathers up the bones,
Like golden straws he gathers them, and a blessing he
intones.

The Hammer now he passeth (though to Etins it brings
strife)
Over Tanngrisnir and Tanngniost and restoreth them to
life.

O, Son-of-Earth, we hail thee when winter coldly
stings;
The Yoole-buck of golden straw Thor's golden blessing
brings!

The holly and the ivy bedeck the merry hall;
Where Mjollnir's might is called upon we shall never
want at all!

The Yule-Goats

The Good Drighten's Hall

Scent you the fires from the good Drighten's hall?
The maid's in the courtyard a-plucking the geese.
The doors of the storehouse are flung to the walls;
Strong lads fill the baskets preparing the feast.
Oh, the scent!
The flesh of the swine!
Can you wait?
How long is the time!
Hear you the sweet tunes that come from the hall?
The minstrels have come for the good Drighten's gold!
Soon will be dancing, and tales to enthrall;
The lyre and the piper shall banish the cold.
Oh, the sound!
The honey-sweet tune!
Can you wait?
We'll call on him soon!
See you the crier the good Drighten sends?
How gaily he's dressed, what good tiding he brings!
"The benches are strewn in the high-timbered hall;
Oh come ye, good people, to feast with the King!"
Oh, the joy!
Abundance delights!
Feast and song
These glad Mother Nights!
Mark ye, good people, our generous lord:
How gracious his table, how cheery the fire!
With silver and cider he brings sweet accord.
Oh sing Yuletide praises for our noble Sire!

The Lighting of the Tree

Generations gather for the lighting of the Tree.
Every branch is gaily clad, so wondrous to see.
O ancient is the column that supports each mighty bough.
A child of Rig, each needle green, Yea, even I and Thou!

Worlds within the branches with many colors shine:
How lovely all together, the garlands fair entwine!
O Tannenbaum doth brighten the winter-weary hall,
For ken that yet a green world sleeps 'neath Holda's downy shawl.

Raise the fragrant balsam, the holy tide to mark:
Every glowing candle helps to chase away the dark.
O Ash and Elm receivéd — more precious, aye, than gold —
The first gifts ever given by three Wise Ones of old!

O none can know the measure of such a mighty Tree.
Each God and Alf and Hero (yea, even you and me!)
Among the countless branches of Yggdrasil we dwell.
Yea, even Asgard shining; yea, even misty Hel!

O Tannenbaum resplendent, bejewelled root to crown,
We raise a merry chorus and gather all around.
Hand in hand, good neighbors, we ring the holy Tree.
May Life and Light and Right Goodwill endure eternally!

Rejoice, O Ye Heathens

Still and cold the morning;
First light breaketh pale.
Fair is Sunna's dawning,
The golden girl we hail.

Rejoice, O ye heathens:
The midwinter is passed.
Where voices glad resound
No darkness long can last.

Sunna in her chariot
Mounts the steely sky.
Hard her stallions labor
To draw her brightness nigh.

Rejoice, O ye heathens,
And look ye to the East.
The triumph of the Light:
For this we sing and feast.

Recall, O ye heathens,
For holy is this day.
Without our golden Lady
The Earth should pass away.

Though e'er the wolf pursueth
And winter grips the land,
All shall be renewéd
By Sunna's blessed hand.

Urd, Verdandi & Skuld

Thor Fishing for the World Serpent

Ned Bates

Riddle

Milky eye of Aurgelmir,
Drawing Aegir's nine daughters to their dance,
Wolf-fled waker of Wode's waxing,
Wolf-fled watcher of womb's waning,
Son of Mundilfari, Midgard's measurer,
Betimes the bearer of his sister's bold brightness
Else a half-shade as Hel
Or masked in midnight's meridian
Awaiting Eostre's rosy embrace.

Fate of the Four

The first lost all taste for life after that night. After her softness, everything felt rough and hard. Her bright tresses had drawn aside like a curtain to reveal a world that was dim and pale. The shine mirrored in her eyes was the swallowed moon. The melody of her laughter had silenced all music, and the depth of her moans had flattened all words so that they crackled in his ears like dead leaves. Her warm wetness had parted for him, but then birthed him into a cold and dry world. And so he became pale and silent. His tools fell from his unfeeling hands, and he sought a distant, lonely crevice where he shriveled slowly into dust.

After reaching such unrivaled heights of physical pleasure, the second sought satisfaction through his tongue and became a glutton. He sought her softness in the flesh of fish and fowl, and her tart sweetness in every variety of wine. Soon his bulging belly pushed him from his jeweler's bench. And then his legs buckled beneath his weight, and he became immobile. Still, he hired servants to bring him his dishes, until one night when his insatiable appetite finally overcame his form, and he burst forth a necklace of innards bejeweled by blood. His last creation.

The third gave into the predilection of his kind and craved gold. The shine and weave of her tresses as they slid through his fingers had left an insatiable mark upon his palm. He took to the mines with a vengeance, sniffing out ore with uncanny ken. He restlessly minted coins, each with her crude effigy, and he counted them endlessly, like the nights since he lay with her. Finally, one fitful night, he hit upon a design for reunion, and pitched himself into the crucible, gilding himself in her tears, and in this way, or so he thought, her affections forever.

The fourth was often found sitting idle, staring up at the night sky, or wandering its shadowed fields, or lying prone among the dark grasses, and thus, among those industrious folk, was thought to have become addle-minded. But how could he explain to them that he had learned to see her face in the moon, to smell her earthy scent in the light caress of nocturnal breezes, to feel her shape against his body when he lay prone in the fields? How could he tell them that for him the night was her shadow, and he her moon-bathed lover?

Notfather

Yip! Yap! What is this place that smells so wet and muddy? Where is the metal tang and branch clang? Where is the mother musk and grunt, the sour nipple milk? And who are you? Are you my father?

Please do not jump on me so, little Yipyap. This place is your new home as deemed by Haptaguth, the god of fetters. Your time with your mother is at an end, but I am not your father. Meat for you from now on, and no more milk. See, I have brought you a cow's haunch for your breakfast.

Yip! Yap! It smells so red and makes a hunger in me. I will eat it soon, but first, O Notfather, will you give me your hand, for I feel afraid in this new place and without my mother whom you say I am never to see again.

This I will do, little Yipyap. Now I scratch your ears, and now scritch your ruff, and now pat your muzzle down.

Yip! Yap! More, Notfather, more scratching and scritching and patting down!

No, little Yipyap. For I am your foster and not your father, and you must not love me overmuch, lest you come to grief anon.

Then, O Notfather, I will eat.

****

Where have you been, Notfather? Can you not see how I have grown? Do you not know the deep, deep hunger that lives within me?

Of course I know your hunger, Yipyap. Was it not I who has fed you these many months? I have brought three brace of oxen to fill your belly.

It is not enough, Notfather! Long has it been since three brace has filled me. I grow and am ever hungry.

On my next visit I will see if more can be spared, but remember you, Yipyap, that others raise the oxen and care for them, and by their hard work is food provided for you. Others must also eat, and oxen have other uses besides.

It is hard to know these things when I am never free of this fen. When you return to your shining hall, can I not go with you and have the bones from your table?

No, Yipyap, this can never be, for Haptaguth has decreed that you are to remain here. Be glad of his mercy, for he is not well known for it.

Trolls take this Haptaguth! Who is he to me? I will not soon forget this doom he dealt. Where is my father? Will he not speak for me or pay a visit? Does he suffer no sorrow at my plight?

No, Yipyap, he will not come, for he is one who does for the sake of doing and dwells not long on consequence. I feel that the next you lay eyes upon him will not be a happy day.

Then trolls take you all! Call me no longer by your pup name, your pet name. Yipyap I am no more. Call me rather Fenwolf if this swampy isle surrounded by sucking mud is to be my home. Let the cows remain, but you take your leave, Notfather.

It is this temper and the hunger behind it that have put you here, Fenwolf. You curse the immoderation of your father, yet you are not less impulsive or unheeding of outcome. I will go and leave you to your bloody repast.

Notfather, wait! Before you leave will you give me your hand? Long will it be ere you return, and no other comes to this desolate place.

This I will do, Fenwolf, for justice needs be dealt without ire if it is to be just. Now I scratch your ears, and now scritch your ruff, and now pat your muzzle down.

Step away, Notfather, for I feel the hunger reaching out its talons for you. Hear its terrible song. Awoooooooo!

****

So, little Notfather, have you and your feeble-hearted companions come to play the game of chains once again? Surely a mightier fetter than the last could not have been forged so quickly? Truth be told, breaking those mighty links made me think that perhaps the strength in my limbs is finally a match for the sucking mud. Perhaps you will find me panting at your hall door on the next moonless night.

And perhaps you hope your bold words will supply the strength you lack. For were you sure of your prowess, you would not be awaiting us here, but would rather be out on the hunt even now. But, such are the bindings I bring today, that besting them will surely prove you ready to brave the muds.

If what you say is not true, it is a cruel jest, indeed.

I think you know well that I speak truly and deal fairly with all, Fenwolf. But this I avow: should you burst these bonds, I know not what could possibly contain you.

What silky ribbon is this? Do you take me for a woman whose hair wants tying?

Unlike those hard-forged links, this cord was smithed by dwarf-magic. Only in this way could a binding be worthy of your might.

I like it not; little I know of witching ways. But how can I be sure when to brave the mud if I cannot best these bonds? Yet how do I know I will be loosed should I fail?

I will give you my hand on it, Fenwolf, against your freedom. A grievous hurt to me should I leave you tied. I place it now in your maw.

Well I know your word, Notfather, so let your lackeys tie their knots and witness the rending of their last hope! Errr, most slippery is this silk, yet the more I strain, the greater it binds. Errr…arooooooo! I am spent. Loose the knots; the isle shall hold me yet.

We will not, Fenwolf, for as you have said yourself, not for much longer can the isle keep you. So bound you stay.

Are you mad? Even now my hunger grows fiercely, loose me before I bite!

Fenwolf, my heart is heavy, but you will stay leashed.

Notfather! Arrrrrrr!

See...see how I have kept to my word, Fenwolf, though it cost me most dear. No such oath could you ever make, for your rage and the hunger behind it would soon make a warlock, an oathbreaker, of you. As your hunger has fated you, so the unbreakable bond of my word has me, and we are thus both brought to grief by our natures.

Say as you will, Notfather. Leashed I may be, but my hunger remains unbound. I will hone my appetite for the day these fetters fail, and then I will devour all, from the most high to the least, until nothing remains but the hunger itself, with only itself to consume. Until then I will have to content myself with the only thing that ever brought me solace. For now I finally have your hand, Notfather, until the end of all things.

The Modern Blind

In ancient time poetic rhyme
Rendered all things person, levels of kind,
From lowly land spirit to gods divine
To whom we owed gratitude, sacrifice, and mind.
But all is inert in the modern blind,
Else pet, lackey, or concubine,
To hew, mow, and mine,
To slaughter, smelt, and bind,
A relentless realm of square and line,
Of mathematics byzantine,
Built on buried refuse, wet with poison, belching grime,
Blunting nature's wax, wane, and wind
All to feed progress's hungry climb
Toward a final end to living time,
All things punished for our crime.

Wave Your Wide Wings, O Mighty Hraesvelgr!

Wave your wide wings, O mighty Hraesvelgr!

The tree branches bow groaning before you,
The plains grasses part in ever-changing paths,
The green seas seethe.
Birds are sent scudding across the sky,
Untied tresses are tossed,
And even buildings can by your wingbeats
Be blown down and broken,
Yet a brave joy rises in the breast of the bold.

Does it anger you when men set their ships' sails against your strength,
And bend mill blades to break grain,
Or when a child cries with joy at a kite's caper?
Do you puff out your feathers with pride at your prowess,
Or do you not notice, knowing us no more than gnats,
Less to you than the carrion you claw into your craw?

Is there joy in your breast when you beat your bounteous wings,
Or red raging wrath,
Or an empty avian mind engaged in an endless chore?

Wave your wide wings, O mighty Hraesvelgr!

Hoard

Do you see yourself as the bold hero? You have dealt a death blow to the greedy beast. But all you wish is to take my treasure in order to make your name legend and advance the politics of your kin. Is this not just another form of greed? Fame-greed. Power-greed.

I was a man once, but I learned that strength and battle prowess fade with age. The joy of women and bed prowess also diminish, and the joys of the hall — drink, games, and banter — eventually lose their luster. But one thing can be held onto as time winds on. One can own. A treasure is a series of stories, the mathom of great deeds. As I turn each sword in my talons, I can hear the clang of its history, the deeds done by it with honor and those treacherous — each famed man whom it bit and bled, each knave laid low in vengeance, each coward's blow hid in the bluster of battle. In every goblet I can taste the one who drank of it — each long-bearded lord; each beautiful maid with wry, red lips; each sly servant taking paltry pleasure downing the dregs. Necklaces sing to me of how they perched boldly above proud breasts, how they were softly strung about eager necks by passionate hands, or collared callously as on an underfoot bitch, or were enfisted in a strangling, jealous grasp. When I lay stretched out upon my hoard, entwining it within my coils, a thousand stories feed my dreams.

How did you think one becomes a dragon? When you own the stories, when you keep the tales, when you prevent them from cycling outwards among the ears and mouths of others, they grow within you. A mere man can not hold such history within him; he must grow greater. His hide grows tougher, a scaled binding for stories unwritten; his fingers grow longer and harder, curving to encircle and hold what is his; his maw widens, his teeth lengthen, that he may devour and ruminate over scores of past deeds, and such knowledge, held silently inside over days, over months, over years, ferments and brews poison. We become our own worlds, serpents with our own tails in our jaws, complete unto ourselves until our loops are lopped by the swords of impudent heroes such as yourself.

So now the treasure is yours in all of its power, glory, and treachery. Enjoy its shine while you may in the short time you have before it consumes you as it did me. For if it does not make a dragon of you, it will devour you in some other fashion. Treasure hoarded will always seek blood until such a time as it is gifted wide and its stories are set free.

O Ancestors Ancient and American

Hail to you, O Ancestors!
To those few whose names and deeds are known to us,
to those many more who are only names,
to the countless whose names we know not,
back to Ask and Embla, whom clever Woden and his
companions carved
from two trunks of branching trees
drifted ashore from the waters of the primordial sea.
Once limbed and breathed to life,
your travels took you the length and breadth of
Midgard;
many shapes and many shades you wore,
many lives and many ways you had,
many worlds dawned and died
as each of you were birthed and then brought to your
bier,
and your children went on to womb new worlds.

Eventually you came here to Vinland's shores,
where the Lady of Liberty would come to stand,
or stood already,
hailing you with her high torch as your ships drew nigh.
You fought for her,
fell for her,
and were laid in the loam of her land.
O, our Ancestors in the American earth.

From many lands we come,
from many mothers, from many fathers,
doubling back through the ages.
We are each a force forged from manifold souls and
myriad deeds.
Each of you lives on in the cellular spiral of molecular
runes

that wove your Wyrd into our very warp and weft.
O, our Ancestors, you are gone, but you are here!
We raise a horn to you:
Hail the Ancestors!

Father of the Slain

In the land of an enemy tribe, a prince lay dying. Strangely, his greatest concern was that his leg was uncomfortably pinned under him from when he fell, unfooted by the force of the enemy shield that had dashed aside his own and allowed through the spear-thrust that was now unmaking him. He struggled briefly to get his leg straightened, but blood was filling his lungs, and soon the labor of breathing consumed him, and the pain and discomfort of his leg faded from his attention. For an unmeasurable amount of time, all became breath and panic, but then he felt a lightening and a shifting, an impossible sense of movement. It was not unlike the feeling he had the night before the battle, when he and his shield brothers had danced around the fire with a spear in either hand, the sacred raven helms upon their brows. They chanted as they leapt and twirled and clashed their spears, until they lost all sense of themselves in the furious movement. That same feeling returned during the earliest moments of the battle, after the first spear had been hurled and the prince and his shield brothers had rushed toward their foes. Despite the weight of his armor and arms, his steps felt light, as if unhindered, and something fierce once again welled up within him and burst forth in a great cry, growing greater as his men took it up, the cry welling against the answering shout of their enemy. It seemed then that he would live forever in that moment, invulnerable and ageless and filled with a boundless, burning fury. These memories brightened the prince's eyes as his labored breath gathered itself and then let loose in a last, long, shuddering sigh. And then he was still.

His company had fled, the enemy host in pursuit. Now the spectators to the battle, the wives and children of the enemy warriors, who during the melee had shouted encouragement to their kinsmen and hurled insults at their foes, swept upon the field to give succor and mourn, to use their knives to finish off any enemy survivors, or to curse and spit upon the enemy dead. An old woman in a blue-black cloak walked among them carrying a staff topped by a small throne upon which sat a wide-eyed effigy. She had been particularly vociferous during the battle, violently waving her thin arms while croaking out spiteful invectives against the enemy, calling for blindness and the binding of limbs. Now she walked to each of the fallen and made pronouncements about his valor in battle — whether his deeds had won his family fame or scarred it with shame. Only after she had spoken over a dead warrior did the mournful family then remove the body. Ravens gathered, perching in nearby trees, gurgling to one another, cocking bright, black eyes toward the fallen warriors.

Soon the families had removed all of their warriors from the field — the dead, the dying, and those of uncertain fate. The fallen enemies were left to lay, except the body of the prince, which was taken as trophy. A few bold ravens then alighted on the edges of the field and hopped tentatively toward the bodies, craning their necks to cautiously peck at wounds before warily hopping backwards. When there was no response, they grew more confident and began to feed in earnest, their more timid comrades circling toward the grim feast. Soon the field was covered in the sheen of blue-black wings and echoed with the scolding croaks of those who squabbled over the tastier morsels.

The wolves came as twilight dwindled to night. They scattered those ravens who had not yet winged off with full bellies, and savaged the corpses. One man who yet lingered, having escaped the knives of the women and children, screamed pitifully as the pack brutally tore at him until he went silent. Then the only sound was the gruesome smack of gorging and the growl and snap of wolfish politics.

The next day the victorious enemy gave thanks by choosing prisoners by lot to be hanged on a tree and then stabbed with a spear. The arms and armor of the fallen foes were broken and defaced and then gifted to the river, blood billowing on the surface as the fame of their deeds was drowned by the depths.

The politics of men, more complex than that of wolves or ravens, but perhaps ultimately just as savage, took longer to unfold in the case of the prince. Negotiations for the return of his body to his people were long and difficult. The feud still burned too warmly for an easy settlement. Eventually the grieving king's frustration grew so great that he disguised himself with a hooded traveler's cloak and thundered out on horseback into the dawning twilight, leading a second horse in train; eight hooves pounding the wet earth. Darkness was falling by the time he reached the foot of a ridge at the edge of his kingdom. The king tied his riding horse to a nearby ash tree, from which he cut a stout limb. Then he lead the second horse, a grey stallion, to the summit. He stood for a moment, overlooking his enemy's domain. Then he drew forth his knife and began to carve runes upon the branch, chanting as he cut. When the entire length of the limb had been scored, the king drove it into the earth, propping it up with stones. He then turned to the stallion, stroking its muzzle to comfort it, whispering apologies. Suddenly, with a swift, practiced blow of his hatchet, he slew the horse. Severing the head with several more hatchet blows, he struggled to lift its unwieldy weight, but finally managed to impale it on the end of the stave. Blood ran down the stave, coloring the runes. The king turned the horse's head to face the rival lands, and then wet his hands upon the blood. Making obscene gestures with his reddened hands, he called forth his grievances to the night, spitting curses toward the land of his foes, while heavy tears of grief and frustration wet his beard. As the eastern sky began to lighten, he finally collapsed in exhaustion. After a time he rose and staggered wearily down the ridge to his riding horse. As he turned and rode for home, the sun broke across the horizon and fell upon the blind eyes of the horse head, which stared unblinkingly toward the enemy as if with silent malediction and woe.

Wrath burns hot, but soon cools, especially if tempered with gold. Even the most stubborn of feuds will often bed down for winter. A settlement between the enemy tribes was eventually made, treasure and prisoners were exchanged, and the body of the prince, now nearly naught but bones, came home. That night a great pyre was built, and his remains laid upon it, adorned with armor, shield, sword and spear, and set alight. The queen and her ladies wailed, honing the edge of their grief which had been dulled with waiting. Armed warriors rode their horses round and round the great balefire and raised cries of mourning and farewell as sparks leapt for the stars.

A feast in the prince's memory was to be held. One evening a poet made his way to the prince's grave. The ashes had been raked into a heap, stones were piled upon it and fresh earth was packed between them and layered on top until it reached a prominent height. On this grave mound the poet sat. He unpinned his cloak, and draped it over his head, blocking out the sights and sounds of the deepening night. He listened silently for a time, and then his muffled song could be heard, trying lines, halting, plying them a different way, pausing to again listen silently, and then singing forth his words anew.

The night of the feast, the prince was hailed with horns of mead and recollected fondly in many a tale. The queen moved among the warriors gathered in the great feasting hall, filling their cups and giving words of welcome and praise. The king, too, lauded his guests and gave gifts. Then the poet plucked his harp sharply and called for everyone's ear, and the hall grew silent. First he sang out the royal lineage, a line begot by a god, but then so sadly cut short. Then he turned to praising the prince, those few bold deeds of a life so brief. The feasters listened and watched the giant shadow of the poet's dancing hands flickering on the hall tapestries; each string-pluck seem to resonate in their hearts, each clever kenning linked the prince's tale to those of the gods and heroes. The poet wove the prince's life into the patterns of the past, into the story of the tribe. The queen paused in her rounds, bowed her head, and turned her back to the company. The king sat on the high seat and silently wept.

Grief is often not long in passing, but some grief lingers, at times leaping unexpectedly to light. Such was the grief of the king and queen. The king sent word for a carver and commissioned a monument to his son. The carver selected a stone and set to work, deftly hammering delicate lines into entwined beasts and swirling serpents, their bellies full of runes. Mistrustful of silent letters and wary of miswordings, he sang out rune names, words, and phrases as they took shape, filling the carved staves with his resonant voice. Once the carving was done, he blew free the bits and set to painting, bringing his beasts alive with bright color and emboldening the runes, singing them once more into the stone. Then the carver sat back, admiring his work. The king would be pleased.

And so the stone sat by the side of a road and told all who passed the tale of the prince's brief fame, even as the king and queen, the poet and the carver, all faded from the earth. Over time the world around the runestone underwent great changes, but the stone aged slowly. Its colors faded, and some runes were rubbed away by the yearly lash of rain and the restless caress of wind. Eventually the rune stone was uprooted and placed in a museum hall, where it riddled scholars and told its fragmented story to new travelers.

Years later, in a far-away country, the runestone unscrolled upon a screen, and a young poet was struck by the sight, a feeling of inspiration welling within him. His fingers began to dance upon a keyboard, lines of words unfurled in shimmering pixels, sometimes reined back and reworded, and a new tale about a long dead prince slowly unfolded into the world.

Jill Evans

Friendship

Dim is the light,
Dark is the night,
But morning meets us daily.
Cool is Fall,
Cold is Winter,
But Spring comes spritely again.
The wheel goes round
To rutted ground,
But turns to the top in time.
Mani wanes,
Then moon goes dark,
But brightest beacon will be.
We say goodnight,
Goodbye, my friend,
But we'll meet again tomorrow.
As with all things,
The wheel still turns
To life and love and laughter.

A Prayer

On Iðavöllr
Ásynjur's Hall
The Friendly Door
For Frigg and all.
The entry framed
In Frith, Kinship
Loyalty, Harvest,
And Hospitality.
Here in Midgard
Men and women
Learn and share
the lore of old.

When pillars fall,
A pile of rubble
May be removed,
May be rebuilt.
May all the Gods,
Goddesses, Disir,
Landvaettir, Alfar,
Aesir and Vanir,
Our Ancestors,
And Einherjar
Help us rebuild
This Hallowed Hall.

A Wish

Black feathered pair in daily flight
Through Ymir's head till last of light:
Oh learnéd fowl of logic and rote,
Whisper of me from Vegtam's coat.

Ravenous hounds of One-Eye's favor,
From head of table his food you savor:
Would I were thusly beside his seat
To glean his wisdom at his feet.

Spider-legged mount, oh trickster's seed,
To Agnar named the highest steed:
With Blusterer over Bifrost ride;
I long to be there by your side.

But only in my sleep scene walk
Or seidr galdr enchanted talk,
By eyes or wolves or ravens black,
I speak to him, he answers back.

Autumn Brings Apples

Ageless are the Aesir
At the onset of Autumn
When Iðunn's sweet apples
Are Iðunn's eternal apples.

Crunchy and juicy,
Crisp as the air:
The yellow fruit of fall,
The yellow fruit of youth.

Dagaz

Here we are in the bright of day:
Odin's messenger
Transforming duplicity
Into Synthesis.
Here is day, and there is night.
Here is black, and there is white.
Here is sadness, and there is joy.
Here is a girl, and there is a boy.
Here is youth, and there is old age.
Here is a fool, and there is a sage.
Here is sweet, and there is sour.
Here is carefree, and there is dour.
Here is soft, and there is rough.
Here is famine, and there is enough.
Here is spring, and there is fall.
Here is a box, and there is a ball.
Here is sun, and there is snow.
Here is the top, and there is below.
Here is flat, and there is steep.
Here is awake, and there is asleep.
Here is a plan, and there is caprice.
Here is anger, and there is peace.
If I seem one, then I am also the other.
And in the middle somewhere,
Collisions. Like Atomic Fusion.
Like the very sun that lights the day.
And the twinkling stars in the dark night.

Ingwaz

Embryonic Image:
Ingwaz brings in Yngvi
To distant soil sailing
To sow a row alone.
Silence wakens senses;
Sounds abound all around.
Awake secret seedling!
Sing in the Spring to Ing!

Jera

Earth's abundant bounty,
Beautiful harvest bar.
Seeds sown after winter
Section for roots and shoots.
The year turns to Jera —
At Yule we'll still be filled.
Gods have granted goodness:
The grain will last again.

Mannaz

Between Earth
And Asgard,
Philosophy
And religion;
Between science
And sorcery
I find Self
And solace.

Community
And countrymen,
Prosperity
Or poverty,
Whether fit
Or feeble,
This is Midgard.
We are Mannaz.

Tiwaz

For seldom seen soldiers,
Sacrifice felt back home.
Twice Tiwaz carved for you.
Tyr I call twice for all.
Young men battled Jotuns;
Yesterday flew away.
Ready today's rally;
Roar victoriously.

Towheaded tot waiting:
Tiny lad misses dad.
A year her heart's yearning:
Youthful bride cries with pride.
Rich are those he reaches,
Roaming no more from home.
Safe, the sounds have ended,
Son, the battle is won.

Perris Zoe Weiland

The Wild Call

Inside my heart there beats a secret drum,
a wild thunder, a roaring hum.

It races across the golden lands,
the deepest seas, the darkest spans.

I feel the call when trapped inside.
An ache for freedom I'm forced to hide.

The sun, the earth, the rain, the sky:
organic fuel to feed my fire high.

What joy I feel to breathe stars to life!
Still, sorrow plagues me,
a sweet, slow, venomous knife.

Few understand this secret I keep.
Fewer still the wanting tears I weep.

My primal body begs to be unbound
when in my heart I hear the lonely sound.

For inside my soul there beats a furious drum,
a wondrous thunder, an unbroken hum.

Idunna

Idunna loves to dance.

She twirls around and around until the hem of her dress catches the breeze. Those carefree doe feet lift her upwards as her arms rise in beautiful supplication to the world tree. I can hear laughter in her smile as she spins beneath Sunna's gentle rays. It always amazes me how she manages to seem so weightless. It's as if she carries no burden at all.

In the depth of the forest where she plays, I find her singing to the woodland creatures there. One by one, she sings to them, songs of love, fertility, peace. Her voice is a songbird's deepest dream. Each note floats with steady gracefulness and would reduce the harshest giants to weeping wool. I watch her when she doesn't expect it. There's a pureness to everything she does. It comes from a heart of literal gold. I'm convinced of it. She wears a crown of flowers upon her wild mane that I don't ever wish to tame. The flowers change with the seasons. Her creatures bring her only the best blooms from across Asgard. Spring flowers are my favorite. Delicate pinks and deep greens weave into a circlet that accents her rosy cheeks. I want so badly to immortalize that look in painting and statue.

I sing to her at night. She always begs me for her favorite songs. "Play me the quick one!" She beams as I grab my instruments and watch her dance around before we retire for bed. Idunna has this infectious inspiration in everything she does. I have yet to see a soul so gorgeous who inspires peace the way she can.

The other gods protect her heavily for she is the bearer of the immortal apples. They come from far and wide across the world tree to have a taste. The crisp, life-renewing fruit gives youth and beauty freely. Just like her. She's so selfless. Always gifting her apples. I think she believes in all the others, everyone who eats the immortal mana. I watch her gift and give all day, hoping that they will stop all this fighting and realize just how precious they are. But they don't hear her sorrow. I try to pretend her optimism comes without a price. But then I would be lying wouldn't I? I've never heard a sadder sound than the tears of my only love. When she weeps, the forest weeps and the apples wilt. I can tell she is tired of it. Tired of the hatred. Tired of the fighting and lies and anger-filled passion and the ecstasy of killing. How could someone so pure in soul and mind understand those concepts? I wish I could protect her from the ugly truth, but in the end all I can do is play the notes her cries make.

I write her sonnets and ballads. She is the object of my fascination. She is a feeling deep inside the fiery pits of my genius. She is the drive and the language of love. My unexpected and eternal muse.

There's nothing to not love about her. From the curves of all her body to the intoxicating enchantment of her personality, she smells like flora and youth and dew. I get lost in the trance of my senses when I am around her. It's effortless. Just like her.

Idunna rolls off my rune-branded tongue and into the hearts of many. The mere idea of her captures the imagination and conjures images of a peaceful world. She loves to dance like the sound of pages turning in your favorite tome or the warm scent of fresh baked pastries around your home. She enraptures. She hypnotizes. She uplifts.

And all I want to do is dance with her.

The Last Valkyrie

Every night the dream is the same.

I look down to find myself dressed in dirty rags this time. I look filthy. I don't think I've bathed in days. The straw of my hut smells of dirty bodies, but it's not as pungent as the stench coming from the summer field beyond the village. I must have slept through the fighting, which is typical of me. I'm a heavy sleeper, or so I'm told. The light filtering through the straw is bright; it must be midday. I walk barefoot across the dirt of the tiny hovel into the open air.

There's death everywhere. Faces of my fellow villagers twisted and contorted into terror. Some were screaming as they died. I used to cry for them, but when you've seen one dead innocent you've seen them all. I grab a pitchfork and shake my head at the irony of this scene. It's like every movie cliché in the history of cinema. The dirty peasant and the pitchfork. I remain unamused and numb to it all. My bare feet carry me mechanically to the field just beyond.

I'm always surprised by the number of dead. I take mental bets with myself on how many I will find this time. I do a quick count. Twenty-seven. A decent amount, considering these men are all wearing heavy plate armor. I poke one with my pitchfork. He seems to be missing his neck, and, judging from the marshy wetness of blood around him, I don't want to turn him over and look. I figure a lot of people probably get queasy imagining what war gore looks like. I know I used to dry heave at the smell when these dreams started. You get used to it, as melancholy as that sounds. I never used to believe the soldiers coming home from war about how it desensitizes you, but it really does.

Time to make the rounds and inspect the bodies. I do it every night, and I don't know why. It's not like any of them are salvable. And if you thought the innocents died gruesomely, you've clearly never seen a warrior-on-warrior wound. Innocents die quickly, and one strike to their soft bodies is normally more than enough to weave their wyrd. But warriors brutalize one another for honor and blood sport. Limbs gone, organs spread everywhere. It's really an impressive display once you get past the horror of it all. Today, I don't see the point in inspection. But there's this voice in my mind that compels me to inspect them anyway. So me and my pitchfork go around poking and prodding. My feet are covered in gore at this point.

A knight sits up as I draw near to him. He looks disoriented and confused. I walk closer to him as he pulls his helmet off and tosses it with anger into the grass. He's handsome and young. All the best warriors from my dreams have strong jawlines and swords. His hair is surprisingly long and blonde. I just stand and watch him rip the clunky armor bits from his shoulders and chest before he finally notices me standing there watching him.

"Good afternoon?" He lifts his brow to me. I can see the wrinkles of stress across his young features quite clearly now.

"Are you hurt?" I kneel down and begin to examine this warrior. He doesn't appear to be bleeding at all. Must have taken a hilt to the dome and gotten lucky he wasn't trampled in the chaos that followed.

"No. I don't appear to be. Just sore. Do you have water?" He frowns, pleading with me.

I pull my leather waterskin from my side and offer it to him, using the pitchfork to balance myself. As he takes it to drink, I look around to see most of the horses are gone or dead. But from the tree line casually strolls the biggest, blackest horse I've ever personally seen. It bears no riding gear, which means it belongs to the village more than likely. It looks like a farmhand breed. I turned my attention back to the knight, who has drained my waterskin.

"Here, take this horse and head north through the forest. You'll reach a village; ask for Hovi. He can get you back to where you need to be." I smile kindly as the horse meanders even closer to us.

After breathing deeply a few times, the knight stood. His bones creak as they are allowed to stretch without the burden of heavy armor.

"Thank you villager. I will remember this kindness." He nods to me in an official sort of way. This was a military man, they all had the same head nod. It was a quick, curt, jerking motion of their chin downwards.

I chuckled, smiling softly as he mounted the horse. All I could do was wave as he rode away without further ado. I sighed, watching him go. I'm not sure who Hovi is, or why I told him to find that person. But it seemed like the right thing to say. All I could do at this point was turn and head back to my slaughtered village.

My eyes open.

Every night the dream is the same.

I look down to find myself dressed in camouflage this time. I feel dusty. The grit of the rocky mountain sands around me has gotten into everything. The heat is overwhelming in all the gear I'm wearing. It's no wonder a common injury in this war is heat stroke. But I wouldn't feel safe without all this gear strapped tightly to my body. The rifle fits just right into the crux of my shoulder for support. My hands cradle its trigger mechanism with perfectly-trained muscle memory.

Carnage once more. These people don't look like me. Their skin is two shades darker. I figure I'm somewhere in the high desert. This village is small, but they always are. The killing looks indiscriminate; there's just a mass of bodies and parts. Normally, you can tell which side was which, but this battlefield is different. There are no distinguishers other than skin color and uniform.

I walk alone through the dry place. Flies are already making their feasts upon limbs, and you can't even smell the rot yet. I think it's toughest when I have to see the children. It doesn't matter what race or religion. In my dreams, the children are always heartbreaking. They don't deserve to suffer in war. Just another thing I have to close my heart to in the end.

The folk are dressed in simple, loose cottons. Their clothing looks handmade. I can practically smell the goat in the threads. I always wondered what it was like to live such a uncomplicated life in some desert village in the mountains of an exotic place. I suppose their lives weren't uncomplicated after all. My heart drops lower into my gut as I approach the epicenter of the carnage.

Bullet holes. Everyone is full of bullet holes.

Why? Why do I keep inspecting these scenes? Why does this strange voice in my mind compel me to carry forward? I shake my head in this high sun when someone catches my eye. A man in robes is sitting peacefully beside a body. His own body. I cautiously walk over to his position; he simply looks up at me and frowns.

"What are you doing?" I demand, pulling my rifle into my shoulder as if to warn him that I will raise it.

He looks at me peacefully and nods, acknowledging the gun in his face.

"I am waiting for Munkar and Nakir."

"Who are they?" I demand, but I get my answers.

Walking towards us are two strange-looking creatures. They have wings and broad shoulders. Their black eyes are visible and distinct. They approach this man. Everything about them radiates power. He stands respectfully, looking around with sad eyes. I can feel his pain. This was his whole village, no one left alive. As these strange men speak, fire comes from their mouths. I can't understand their words, but this man seems to. They ask him three questions, and apparently his responses are satisfactory because he suddenly smiles, and one of the creatures escorts him away. The other creature looks at me and nods his head. I stare, mesmerized at this being as it turns to follow the other two. It isn't often I see anyone else in these dreams who isn't a soldier of some kind. Who are they? I ask myself. They seem so familiar. The sound of helicopter blades overhead jerks me out of my trance.

"Slippy this is Valkyr Bravo. We've got one. Over."

I move quickly to one of mine. He's sitting up with an amount of difficulty outside a hut. I rush over to help him stand as the bird starts to lower to our position.

"What happened? The insurgents came…I…Ah…" He grips his head as the sun pierces his eyes forcing him to squint in order to see me properly. "Rogers. Martinez. Dulle. There were kids in this village! They just opened fire on us all…Did…did anyone make it?" He looks to me hopefully.

I just smile at him as the bird lands and the bay doors open up for him.

"Go on soldier. Slippy'll take ya to General Forni for orders. We got this place covered," I reassure him.

He nods to me in an official sort of way. This was a military man. They all had the same head nod. It was a quick, curt, jerking motion of their chin downwards. Then he took off into the waiting arms of the helo and up into the sky.

Once he was away, I turned to check the hut behind me. And sure enough, cowering on the floor in the darkness of a small building was a child. The only child to have survived this massacre. She didn't look scared of my uniform. She just waved at me as tears of innocent mourning fell down her face. I wanted to reach out and say something.

My eyes open.

Every night the dream is the same.

I look out among the blood-soaked sheepskin and leather. Disemboweled bodies with axes still stuck in their guts was not a sight for the faint of constitution. The smell was bad here. The grass beneath this mass of bodies was just gore for the raven's feast.

My leather boots were clean as I strode gracefully into this field. There were no villages around for miles. This was a score to settle between two dueling earls. I watch, draped in thick warrior's leathers, wielding my spear. And soon, four men sit up. They look dirty and aged from combat. Wrinkles formed around their eyes and mouths. Blood stained their faces.

"Ulfnar. Harthir. Bijarke. Hagen."

These men all stand with creaking joints and look at me. One by one, smiles spread across their faces. I feel someone move behind me. He wears dark robes and a raven on his shoulder. His one-eyed smile greets me like an old friend. I turn as he addresses me.

"You have chosen well. I will take them from here."

I turn to look back at the men who are slowly walking towards us.

"Follow Odin for Valhalla." I gesture as the old man turns to walk off into the forest line and lead the faithful to his hall.

My eyes open.

Eirik Westcoat

Snowfall Across the Worlds

All the events in the upper worlds,
even if ordinary, influence Midgard.
Mother Frau Holle is making her bed,
shaking her blankets, shaking them vigorously,
and *we* get a blanket of the whitest snow.
The continual din of the day is tapered,
sound is suffocated, by that snow-blanket,
and pure silence peals in powerful waves
across Midgard. We come to a halt,
our frenzy suspended in a forced rest,
an opportunity to take the measure
of our being and time 'gainst boundless nature.
The simple action of an ancestral goddess:
so commonplace, occurring frequently,
yet miraculous ever. Really, how else
could the wondrous worlds thus work together?

The Six Treasures

Bölverk's bounty
I bear tonight
and pour a portion to share.
I tell a tale
of treasures six,
owned by our awesome gods.

The beautiful locks
of alluring Sif
were sheared by mischief's maker;
Thor was wroth,
raged at Loki,
demanded he find a fix!

Then Loki wended
to the world of Dwarves;
their skill he schemed to hire.
The smiths began,
the sons of Ívaldi:
Goldlocks they gleamingly shaped.

The smiths continued,
the sons of Ívaldi:
Skíðblaðnir they skillfully shaped.
The smiths finished,
the sons of Ívaldi:
Gungnir they grimly shaped.

Then Loki wended
to wager with Brokk
against the greatness of treasures.
A swine's skin
by skillful Eitri
was forged to gleaming Gullinbursti.

Glowing gold
by gifted Eitri
was forged to dearest Draupnir.
Blazing iron
by brilliant Eitri
was forged to foe of etins,
was forged to mighty Mjöllnir.

Brokk was steady,
on bellows he stayed,
the scheme of the fly he foiled!
Treasures he took
to try in Asgard,
Aesir joining in judgement.

Óðinn and Thor,
and third was Freyr,
the gods who joined in judgement.
The given verdict,
the greatest treasure:
best was bane of etins,
best was mighty Mjöllnir!

Thor Processional Chant

Great Thor, Thor, Thor,
the thunderer we hail,
that greatest son of Gaut.
We celebrate now
this son of earth
for all his great good gifts.

Ásabrag we hail,
the Aesir lord,
that greatest god of karls.
That warder of workers
gives weal unto all
where oak or rowan rises.

For Man in Midgard
he's a mighty defender
who hallows and holds our shrines.
For Man in Midgard
he's a mainful patron
who furthers the fecund earth.

Eindriði we hail,
and onward he strives
to ward the worlds 'gainst etins.
Gjálp and Greip
and Geirröð, too,
he ended to aid the worlds.

For Man in Midgard
he's a mighty defender
who hallows and holds our shrines.
For Man in Midgard
he's a mainful patron
who furthers the fecund earth.

Harðhugað we hail,
his heart is greatest:
his boldness boosts our courage.
He slew Hrungnir
to hold them safe,
the Bonds and their boons in Asgard.

For Man in Midgard
he's a mighty defender
who hallows and holds our shrines.
For Man in Midgard
he's a mainful patron
who furthers the fecund earth.

Hlórriði we hail
for the help he gives
that blesses our fertile fields.
The rain he brings
in righteous downpours,
by thunder from mighty Mjöllnir.

For Man in Midgard
he's a mighty defender
who hallows and holds our shrines.
For Man in Midgard
he's a mainful patron
who furthers the fecund earth.

Véurr we hail,
that valiant warder
of Midgard's mighty shrines.
Both barrow and vé
he blesses and holds,
hallowing the runes we write.

Hail the hallower
— that holy warder —
hail to Thor, Thor, Thor!
Hail the Great One
— that glorious Ás —
hail to Thor, Thor, Thor!

Öfundarmál

The towering Tree
is topped by an eagle
who scorns the serpent
for scores of slights.
Haughty, headstrong,
and highfalutin,
that proudest bird
is puffed up well.

Deep in the roots
a dragon lurks,
bitter with bile,
biting corpses.
Sour and surly
(with searing hate
for that damned eagle),
the dragon smolders.

Both up and down,
an acorner runs
along the trunk
of that lofty tree.
He whisks the words
of the wyrm and eagle
both back and forth,
those bitter insults.

Now you may hear
some nuggets of speech
that pass between
those prideful ones,
in reading here thus
the runes of the squirrel;
be wary of finding
that woe within.

The Eagle said:
"Scurry my squirrel,
and scamper quickly;
let that serpent slime
hear slanderous words.
Supreme I am
o'er the piddly snake
because my view
reveals all knowledge."

The Serpent said:
"Scurry my squirrel,
and scamper quickly;
let that 'carry-on' bird
hear accusing words.
I lord o'er realms
that lout can't see;
I simply don't value
the view he has."

The Squirrel said:
"The saw he said
is slander surely,
O wisest wight
of worlds all nine.
That jerk deserves
rejoinders many;
repay his gift
with a prideful 'gild."

And so it goes,
that senseless gab.
Can the hapless hawk
give help at all?
Where is the tree
of this wisdom tale?
Can Elm or Ash
offer assistance?

The Brísingamen

Might with metals
is the main of dwarves,
and as good as any
are Grérr, Álfrigg,
Dvalinn, and Berling
in doing that work.
In a rock they lived
and wrought their craft.

Word of their work
had wended far,
flying to Asgard
and Freyja's ears.
In a day of wandering,
the Dís of the Vanir
came in the cave
of these crafty dwarves.

The eyes of Freyja
then angled upon
a gleaming necklace
of gold and amber.
'Twas Brísingamen,
the best of jewels,
and Fólkvang's lady
was flaming with lust.

The greatest treasure
of gold and silver
she offered to them
to own that jewel.
But the dwarves declined
and deemed her money
a rather poor price
for parting with it.

The craftsmen then
declared their price:
her body would be
the best exchange.
In love and lust
she'd lay with them
for one night each
to win that jewel.

For nights all four,
her nubile form
sated the lust
of salacious dwarves;
furtively then
Freyja returned,
back to her bower
with the beautiful jewel.

But Loki had witnessed
that long exchange
of carnal delights,
craving mischief.
As with Sif before,
he would seek a way
to slip inside
and seize her treasure.

Alone at night,
Loki then searched.
In form of fly
he flitted around,
hoping to find
a hole to enter.
Up by the gable
he gained his entrance.

Freyja was found
by Farbauti's son,
soundly sleeping
inside her bower.
Above her breast
was Brísingamen;
beneath her neck
was the needed clasp.

Into form of flea
the feisty one
then changed and bit
her cheek with malice.
Startled she stirred,
then stretched and turned.
The clasp exposed,
he carried it off.

When morning came,
Mardöll awoke
and noticed now
her necklace gone.
Unbroken but open
was her bower door.
Was it Byleist's brother
who'd been inside?

To the hall of Hár
she hastened for news,
asking if any
had answers to give.
Where was Loki
or the winsome jewel?
The gathered Aesir
together mooted.

The sly one was seen
sneaking away,
carrying something
he was keeping hidden.
Whither went he
wending quickly?
Silent Víðarr
to Singasteinn pointed.

On hearing that news,
Heimdall the White
stood and started
and stammered almost.
As warden of Bifröst
he watches the realms,
yet mischief's maker
he'd missed completely.

The son of sisters
then sought to redeem
his failure of sight
by finding the thief.
Great Gullintanni
would regain that jewel,
his service pledged
to Sýr for honor.

Valiant Vindlér
ventured to Singasteinn,
a skerry far out
and scoured by winds.
To reach that rock,
from radiant Ull
he received a bone
to surf the waves.

A seal was swimming
in the sea nearby,
splashing around
in sparkling water.
A shape-shifter
he'd surely found,
Sýr's servant knew,
on seeing its eyes.

The burly brute
then barked in anger
when he realized
the watchman saw him.
Under the waves
he went and vanished,
leaving Heimdall
alone on the rock.

But Heimdall was skilled
in the hidden magics
and knew the charms
to change his shape.
He rowned some runes
in a rhythmic chant;
to shape of seal
he shifted his form.

In the drink he dove,
down after the fiend,
flapping flippers
in furious pursuit.
The warrior warden
in water moved quick
and nearly caught
crafty Nálarson.

Loki evaded
and leapt on the rock
to face and fight
his furious pursuer.
The bouncing blubbers
in battle then crashed,
a serious struggle
on Singasteinn.

Heimdall with his head
then hammered Loki.
It served him well
as a sword of might,
for the top of his tree,
containing authority,
availed against Loki
for victory on the rock.

Byleist's brother
was beat at last;
regained for Gefn
was the gleaming jewel.
Loki was bound
and led back home.
Heimdall's honor
was healed through glory.

Now that necklace
is on noble Freyja;
it brightens her beauty,
that best of jewels,
for Mardöll is honored
by mighty treasures,
that glorious mother
of Gersemi and Hnoss.

A Tale of Wisdom's Well

Now wisdom's way I praise
— 'tis Woden's holy road —
with mead I rightly made
from might of lore tonight.
Deeply drink — don't just sip —
this draught of main and gain
in hearing tell of Hár,
on how and why that eye!

First had Búri got Borr.
Then born was Ölvir-Forn:
from a crude corpse he made
what's called our home by skald.
Hanging high, nine nights long,
beholding runes as boons,
this gloried god went far
but glimpsed much more in store.

To get seið-skill he sought
sensuous Freyja then:
ecstasy alters luck.
Through herbs no rot perturbs
the head of Hœnir's bud:
hidden tales it unveils.
They're not enough to quaff:
he needed more of lore.

Wanting to gain he went
for wisdom to be his;
under the Ash he'd wend
by Etin-home and roam
along a root so right
to reach and then beseech
a dram from master Mím:
a mighty trip that sip!

Then grimly Gaut hailed Mím
who, grand with horn in hand,
refused the fuel he prized:
for free it would not be!
A price instead he paid,
a part most dear and near:
to have that gulp he gave
a globe of sight that night.

For gain his eye was gone;
then Gjallarhorn was borne
— deeply undimmed it beamed —
with draught so full of craft.
Crystal clear was its fire;
no clouds stained or remained
in sky of Skollvald's will:
screaming bright, yet no dream.

That member he gave Mím
is mighty still in sight:
rowning of realms unseen,
right it dwells in the wells.
He's stirred to understand
through strength of both at length;
much wisdom deep he draws
from draught and eye of craft.

Onward ever he'll run,
aiming for more to claim
of wisdom wild and bold:
wode for his holy road!
Honor his eye and boon,
for always they recall
that feat of glory great
for Gods and Men to ken.

Yggdrasilsdrápa

From trees are made
us true heathens,
and I seek silence
for singing my praise
of that tallest tree
— truly mighty —
that holds the homes
and is hight Yggdrasil.

From its drops of dew,
a draught I brew
of Ygg's ale now
and open that flow
to stir with words
our wode tonight.
Drink now deeply
this draught of skalds.

Of trees it is best
and I truly name
the nine bright worlds
that needle-ash bears.
The North has Niflheim
and its numbing Ice.
The South has Muspellsheim
and its searing Fire.

The West has Vanaheim,
the world of the Vanir.
The East has Jötunheim,
the Etins' home realm.
Above is Ljósálfheim,
the blessed realm of Elves.
Below is Svartálfheim,
the land of the Dwarves.

Highest is Asgard,
home of the Aesir.
Lowest is Hel,
the land of the Dead.
But Midgard for Man
is in the middle of all.
Now hight are the worlds
that hang on that Tree.

With worlds all nine,
that Wood does shine.
Always that Tree
evergreen shall be.

That Tree rises
from roots and wells;
three each it has,
its thirst they quench.
A root in Hvergelmir
— that roiling cauldron —
provides it the power
of primal nature.

A root in Mímisbrunn
— that Mímir watches —
stores the matter
of memory and wisdom.
A root in Urðarbrunn
— the realm of the Norns —
accumulates the wyrd
that works in the Tree.

From the wells it needs
those waters and deeds.
Always that Tree
evergreen shall be.

Burdened with beasts,
it bears them well.
A stately eagle
stands at the top,
Níðhögg beneath
gnaws on the roots,
and Ratatosk with gossip
runs between them.

Hungry harts four
harrow it also.
Numberless serpents
slither beneath it.
In farthest future
the fire of Surt
will burn the Tree's
trunk and branches.

That harm and thrash
hinders the Ash.
Though trials arrive,
the Tree will survive.

Near Urðarbrunn
the Norns do dwell.
The first is Urð
of formative past.
The second is Verðandi
of ceaseless becoming.
The third is Skuld
of threatening due.

With water and mud
they wet the Tree
to keep away
decay and rot,
and they lay layers
for life in the Well;
their faithful work
furthers that Tree.

With wyrd they heal
that Wood's ordeal.
Though trials arrive,
the Tree will survive.

But the best of burdens
it bore of old
when the Aesir's lord
— eager for wisdom —
sought the mysteries
and mounted that Steed
for nights all nine
of needful riding.

Thund was hanging
in thirst and hunger
from high branches
with harrowing wound
to gain by ordeal
a glimpse of death;
thus as gallows
the great Tree served.

The Worker of Wode
wanted the power
that was offered only
by the awesome Runes.
With a final scream
he fulfilled his quest
and lifted at last
their lore from the Tree.

Great Yggdrasil
is always green,
despite the burdens
that would break its spirit;
that source of life
and sacred lore
is ever deserving
of honor and praise.

May Elm and Ash
give ear to these words:
Outside and in,
Yggdrasil is real,
and may this mead
give might to both —
to the Tree without,
to the Tree within!

End Matters

Selected Performances & Publications

Ned Bates

- "Fate of the Four" — Trothmoot 2015 Skaldic Competition Winner. The piece has also been performed at ECT.

Ristandi

- "John Greycap" has been performed at ECT.

Mike Smith

- "Óðinn" has been performed at ECT.
- "Runic Rowner" has been performed at ECT.

Jesseca Trainham

- "The Yule-Goats" — ECT 2018 Art Competition, 2nd place.

Eirik Westcoat

- "The Six Treasures" — ECT 2011 Skaldic Competition Winner, Spoken Word.
- "Yggdrasilsdrápa" — ECT 2012 Skaldic Competition Winner, Poetry.
- "A Tale of Wisdom's Well" — ECT 2013 Skaldic Competition Runner Up, Spoken Word.
- "Thor Processional Chant" was first used in ritual at ECT 2016.
- "Snowfall Across the Worlds" first appeared at <www.theskaldiceagle.com>. Eirik's other poems were previously published in his *Viking Poetry for Heathen Rites* (2017). "Öfundarmál" and "A Tale of Wisdom's Well" were also published the Troth's *Idunna* 96 (Summer 2013) and *Idunna* 97 (Autumn 2013), respectively.

Biographies

Ned Bates has a BA in Literature and Anthropology, an MFA in Creative Writing, and is a public school teacher and writer. He has made a life's study of the places where objective and imaginative worlds meet, and is especially fascinated by the collision of modern and ancient worlds and the creative work inspired by the resulting plurality and syncretism of world-views. He is a heathen who seeks to balance reconstruction of ancient ways, pragmatism, and poetry. His fiction has appeared in *Ex Libris*, Boston University's former literary journal. He has presented his fiction, nonfiction, and poetry at East Coast Thing, Trothmoot, and The Polytheist Leadership Conference, and erratically blogs as the Heretical Heathen: <hereticalheathen.blogspot.com>.

Jill Evans has been part of the Northeast Heathen Community since about 2006 and is a member of Glitnir Kindred. She has lived in the Lehigh Valley in Pennsylvania for the last 30 years. She currently lives with her husband of 36 years, adult daughter, three dogs, and two cats. She holds a BS in Engineering Technology with an emphasis in Mechatronics from Temple University.

Stephanie (Conrod) Janicedottir is a long-time New England native who discovered the Norse Gods as a teenager when a relative gave her a copy of Padraic Colum's *The Children of Odin*. Going to UMass in the early 90s, she joined the UMass Pagan Students Organization and met the founding members of Raven Kindred. She professed to Asatru in 1993 and joined Raven Kindred shortly after that. Following graduation in 1997 and a short-lived marriage, Stephanie went "into the woods" and pursued a solitary practice. After the birth of her second child in 2003, Stephanie met Mike and Cat Burke-Smith, who invited her to become a founding member of the Úlfar aff Jera Þjóð. She has been active in the local NEHC for over two decades.

Laurel Mendes is a current member of Gladsheim Kindred and a former member of Hrafnar Kindred. She has been in continuous practice of our faith and the various magical arts of our ancient kin of faith for more than 30 years. Starting in 1989, she was an integral part of Hrafnar's work to recreate the Spae rite of our ancient kin of faith. She has been practicing, teaching, and learning ever since. Today, she lives in Baltimore with her husband and her beloved cats, and spends her spare time doing what she loves most: cooking, writing poetry, and singing.

Ristandi has been part of the Northeast Heathen Community since he relocated to New England in 2008. A Master in the Rune-Gild (which he joined in 1993) and member of its standing High Rede, he's been attending ECT for nearly a decade. He's also a professional songwriter and lyricist and has written or performed on 13 albums to date. He currently teaches at a small private college in the Green Mountains.

Mike Smith has been an open, public member of the Ásatrú and heathen community for over 28 years. Once a member of Raven Kindred North in the mid-1990's, he left to be the founder of Athelingúlf Fellowship, which, upon moving to New Hampshire, evolved into the Úlfar aff Jera Þjóð in 2005. Over the years, he has written many articles, participated in Pagan Pride Days, and is a regular presenter at East Coast Thing since its inception in 1999.

Jesseca Trainham has been a working artist since graduating *magna cum laude* from SUNY Potsdam in 2001 with a BA in Studio Art. She has hand-crafted Heathen sacred art on wood since 2006, establishing a devoted following first on eBay, and now on Etsy as seller Lady Buckthorn. Her illustrations have been featured most notably in Brian Smith's *Gerímbóc: The Anglo-Saxon Calendar* and in *The Words of Odin*, Robin Artisson's translation of the Hávamál. Eirik Westcoat's own *Viking Poetry for Heathen Rites* also features her distinctive pyrography as cover art. A member of the Oswego-based Úthellingu Kindred, Jesseca is proud to have created the promotional art for CNY's Pagan Pride event since 2015, and maintains the Sunna vé at ECT. Jesseca resides in a quirky old farmhouse in Scriba, NY with her cherished husband Brian, 3-legged cat Buddy, and guinea pig, Mr. Pickles.

Perris Zoe Weiland has been a heathen since 2014 and is a current member of the Northern Virginia / DC Kindred Mannaheim. She served in the United States Marine Corps and is a decorated combat veteran. She is Polynesian with a family history of Native Hawaiian, an active member of the LGBTQ community, and the only female featured in the documentary *American Jedi*. She has written for several prominent publications and is currently working as a freelance contractor for video games such as *World of Warcraft* and *Skateboard Sushi*. Perris is an internationally certified hypnotist and skincare expert among other distinguished awards. She is currently a student of the volva arts, with a seminary graduate background from both Christianity and Eastern Philosophy. Her Vanic passions and views are reflected heavily in her Heathen practice and writing.

Eirik Westcoat is a long-time Asatruar who has presented his award-winning poetry at several regional Asatru gatherings in the American Northeast. He writes mainly in Old Norse and Old English poetic meters. He has published two books: *Viking Poetry for Heathen Rites* (2017), a book of Asatru religious poetry, and *Eagle's Mead* (2019), a book of esoteric initiatory poetry and prose. He is a Master in the Rune-Gild, and that latter book presents a rare poetic look at the process of runic initiation. He also has written articles on the Old Norse *galdralag* poetic meter and the meaning of the valknut.

www.ingramcontent.com/pod-product-compliance
Lightning Source LLC
Chambersburg PA
CBHW032034130726
48284CB00008B/2580

* 9 7 8 1 9 4 7 4 0 7 1 2 1 *